Institute of Education
UNIVERSITY OF LONDON

Review of Recent Research on the Achievement of Girls in Single-Sex Schools

JANNETTE ELWOOD AND

CAROLINE GIPPS

First published in 1999 by the
Institute of Education University of London,
20 Bedford Way, London WC1H 0AL
Tel: 0171-580 1122. Fax: 0171-612 6126

Pursuing Excellence in Education

© Institute of Education University of London 1999

British Library Cataloguing in Publication Data:
a catalogue record for this publication is available
from the British Library

ISBN 085473 590 9

Produced in Great Britain by
Reprographic Services
Institute of Education University of London

Printed by Formara Limited
16 The Candlemakers, Temple Farm Industrial
Estate, Southend on Sea, Essex SS2 5RX

I1/0005-PEP No.5-0599

90 0410415 6

REVIEW OF RECENT RESEARCH ON THE ACHIEVEMENT OF GIRLS IN SINGLE-SEX SCHOOLS

CONTENTS

vi   Foreword

1   Introduction

2   Background

3   Academic performance

4   Academic performance from an
    international perspective

5   School and social factors

6   Summary, conclusions and future
    research agenda

7   References

FOREWORD

This fifth publication in the Perspectives on Education Policy series, by Jannette Elwood and Caroline Gipps, brings a much-needed research perspective to the controversy about whether girls achieve better results in single-sex schools.

The issue arouses strong emotions in advocates of single-sex education for girls and in those for whom comprehensive schooling implies co-education. Although this work was funded by the Association of Maintained Girls' Schools, it provides an admirably impartial review of the latest research evidence. Making sense of the data on achievement is difficult when many single-sex girls' schools have had a history of academic and social selection. The authors conclude that the case for the academic superiority of girls' schools remains 'not proven', but they also point out that academic achievement is not the only reason for arguing for or against single-sex education for girls.

While this monograph focuses on the achievement of girls in different types of school, it is also relevant to more general debates about the apparent 'under-achievement' of boys in recent years and to more specific arguments about single-sex teaching in mixed schools.

PROFESSOR GEOFF WHITTY
Dean of Research, Institute of Education

April 1999

Preface

This review of research was funded by the Association of Maintained Girls' Schools (AMGS). The authors would like to thank the AGMS for their sponsorship and help throughout the course of this project. We would especially like to thank Joan Senior (Honorary Secretar of AMGS) and Jane de Swiet (President of AMGS) for their guidance and support in the writing and production of this research review.

1
Introduction

Gender-related differences in performance, and particularly differences in achievement, have generated much attention and debate since the early 1980s. This interest in the comparative patterns of boys' and girls' results covers the whole range of testing in the British educational system – from differential performance in national curriculum assessment for seven year-olds to variations in male and female success rates at university degree level (Elwood, 1995). Of particular concern over the last few years has been the perceived underachievement of boys, particularly at GCSE. Media coverage of examination result patterns and league tables in the UK have made much of this concern (e.g. 'The Future is Female', Panorama, BBC TV, November 1994: Bright, 1998;

Lepkowska, 1998). Furthermore the Chief Inspector of Schools regards the under-achievement of boys as 'one of the most disturbing problems we face within the whole education system' (Chris Woodhead, *The Times*, 6 March 1996).

More generally, we seem to be witnessing a sense of moral panic about the underachievement of boys and their lack of opportunity to do well (Pyke, 1996). However, girls are still being 'blamed' in some way for boys' failure: critics have suggested that the legacy of equal opportunities policies to enhance equality of access and resources have benefited girls more than boys. Schools in their eagerness to encourage girls' achievements have neglected boys'. The revolution of girls' education set in motion by equal opportunities policies, has been seen to be responsible for the demoralisation of boys (Judd, 1994). However, we have yet to understand fully the impact of such perspectives on boys' and girls' achievement. What is clear is that deficit models of equal opportunity which 'blame' any one group are counter-productive to providing a better experience for all pupils.

This sense of moral panic that is portrayed in the media, and the inaccessibility of some academic research, have led to conflicting messages for teachers, governors, policy makers, parents and inspectors. One such simplistic message is that it is all boys who are underachieving and all girls are outperforming boys. However, the situation is more complex and raises the important and critical questions of which girls, at what stages of their education, and according to what criteria are they presumed to be outperforming boys? There is also a widespread belief that stems from the publication of school league tables that girls from single-sex schools are performing best across all phases of compulsory and post-compulsory education. However, even within the category of single-sex girls schools there is a variety of type of school and patterns of performance within these schools, with different intakes, all of which have been shown to affect performance (Smithers and Robinson, 1995, 1997).

This report presents an up-to-date review of the recent research literature on the achievement of girls in single-sex schools. Parallel to the main issue of achievement of girls in these schools are the debates about single-sex versus mixed-sex schooling in general, the social and academic environments of single-sex schools and their effect on girls' performance, and the growing popularity of single-sex classes in mixed-sex schools that have been established to counteract some of the gender-related performance differences observed. Within the review it is acknowledged that at some of the most important stages of schooling in the UK, the performance patterns of boys and girls are changing, the old stereotypes no longer hold firm and that we are looking at new complexities in performance for the late 20th century and beyond. The review aims to highlight the main findings in the most recent research and to encourage informed debate on the issues of girls' achievement in single-sex schools.

2
Background

Smithers and Robinson (1997) suggest that the publication of performance tables for schools has revived the old debate about whether it is better for girls, and indeed boys, to be taught in separate schools. Many of the schools at the top of the school performance tables are single-sex schools from both the maintained and independent sectors and many of them are girls-only schools. The re-emergence of the interest in single-sex schooling in relation to the school performance tables has coincided with a renewed interest in general about the most appropriate organizational arrangements for girls' and boys' schooling at the secondary level. The interest ranges from radical conservatives and feminists finding common ground in their expression of reservations about coeducation (Daly, 1996), to a concern at the general decline in the provision of single-sex schooling in both the independent and maintained sectors (Smithers and Robinson, 1997). Of those who advocate the retention and promotion of single-sex schooling most are proponents of this type of schooling for girls. As Daly (1996) suggests, higher expectations appear to be widely entertained for academic achievement and social development by advocates of single-sex schooling for girls to the extent that economic and socially driven policies associated with coeducation are being re-examined.

Leonard (1996) reminds us that the UK has had a very long history of single-sex education for all age groups, but that it has been particularly marked among elite groups such as public schools, grammar schools and the Oxbridge colleges. It has also been associated with concerns for religious education especially in England, Wales and Northern Ireland where many catholic and Anglican schools continue with single-sex schooling for both boys and girls. Much of the state schooling in the UK, up to and including the time of the 1944 education reform act, was single-sex (Smithers and Robinson, 1997). Most of the grammar schools created after the 1944 act were single-sex. It was thought natural to separate the sexes at the secondary level of education as boys and girls were being prepared for different roles: boys were being prepared to be husbands and for work and girls to be wives and mothers and for work in the home.

It was the work of R. R. Dale (1969, 1971, 1974) that first began to stress the benefits of coeducation for both the sexes. Dale's work was carried out in the wake of government directives for local authorities to set up comprehensive school systems. Leonard (1996) suggests that coeducation, thought to be a more progressive form of secondary schooling was brought in 'on the coat-tails of comprehensivisation' (p.21). The drive towards providing equal opportunity for all pupils saw state schools being reorganized into coeducational establishments that did not segregate pupils by ability, sex, race or religion (Smithers and Robinson, 1997). Dale's work (op. cit.) on English and Welsh secondary schools stressed how much better coeducation was, particularly in social terms and particularly for the achievement of boys. He expressed cautiously in his overall conclusion that girls' progress was not harmed by coeducational schooling (Daly 1996) and that, in fact, mixed schooling provided 'optimal adjustment to life for all its students' (Gill, 1993:91).

The consequence of greater comprehensivization and the creation of coeducational schools was the major reduction in the number of single-sex schools, especially in the state sector (Smithers and Robinson, 1997). Recent data from The Equal Opportunities Commission and Ofsted (EOC/Ofsted, 1996) shows that there are now only 227 single-sex girls' schools and 197 single-sex boys' schools left in the state secondary sector where there had been over 2,000 single-sex schools in the late 1960s and early 1970s (Smithers and Robinson, op. cit.). The scale of this reduction has made single-sex state schools feel extremely threatened. Smithers and Robinson (1997) also show that there has been a similar shift in the independent sector but not quite on the same scale. They report that while in 1968 only three of the 273 independent schools were coeducational, by 1997 almost 290 of the 580 institutions described as independent were coeducational.

Similar trends have been found in the USA and Australia (Sadker and Sadker, 1993; Gill, 1993). Gill (1993) has reviewed the Australian research literature on the single-sex versus coeducational debate. She noted that the number of single-sex girls' schools in the public (state) sector had decreased considerably. At the time of her review there were no public sector single-sex girls' schools in four of the Australian states. As in the UK, there had been a decline in the number of single-sex schools in the private sector but the decline was less marked than in the state sector.

In the USA, single-sex education has been illegal in many states from around 1972 (Sadker and Sadker, 1993). While some single-sex schooling survives in the independent sector, virtually all of the state sector is coeducational. Again, coeducational schools in the USA were set up under the auspices of equal opportunity programmes for all pupils. However, groups such as the American Association of University Women have taken a critical look at the effects of coeducation on girls' schooling and achievement and they have suggested that the issue of boys' and girls' schooling in the USA needs to be rethought (AAUW, 1992, 1998).

Similar concerns to those voiced by the AAUW in the USA have been voiced for many years by feminist educators in the UK who from the late 1970s and early 1980s have contested the general consensus around coeducation. They assert that single-sex schools are actually better for girls and that girls achieve better academic results in single-sex schools (Leonard, 1996). Shaw (1976) was one of many British educators who reported on the heels of Dale's work, that in fact, girls' academic achievement appeared to be closely linked to school type, with the high achievers coming from single-sex schools. Other educators were keen to point out that girls were more likely to undertake maths and science in girls' schools even though such schools tended to be less well equipped in these areas than mixed schools (Bone, 1983). The paradox generated from these early discussions is that many educators (mainly feminist educators) were convinced that girls were better off being educated in girls' schools while boys were better off being educated in coeducational schools (Arnot, 1983; Deem, 1984; Spender, 1980).

In 1983, the Equal Opportunities Commission in the UK commissioned a major piece of research into girls and their achievements in girls-only schools (Bone, 1983). This work was a large-scale review of all the evidence to date on single-sex and coeducational schools and the achievements of girls in both these types of schools. The research carried out by Bone investigated the evidence both for and against the claims that girls in girls-only schools perform better in examinations, feel freer to chose a wider range of subjects and therefore to follow careers that do not conform to a feminine stereotype and that open up wider fields of employment. From her analysis Bone concludes:

> the subject mixes taken by girls, their academic results and the responses of schools to their more personal needs have been conditioned far more by the type of school they attend (comprehensive, grammar, modern or independent) and the style of the school (traditional or not) than by whether their school was single-sex or mixed. The repeated absence of a strong indication in favour of either a girls-only environment or a mixed environment through the great variety of research reviewed supports the conclusion that this aspect of schooling on its own has not been crucial.
>
> (Bone, 1983:1-2)

Almost 15 years later in the most recent report published on this topic, Smithers and Robinson (1997) reinforce Bone's conclusions. They report that it is still difficult to substantiate whether one type of schooling is better than the other. In their earlier report, *Coeducation and Single-Sex Schooling* (1995), they analysed schools' examination results for the 1994 examination session. Their conclusions in this report reiterated Bone's (1983) in that single-sex schools topped the school performance tables for reasons associated with 'single-sexness' rather than the segregation of the sexes itself. Single-sex schools differ from coeducational schools in important ways besides admitting only either girls or boys. They tend to be highly selective in terms of their intake, recruit from higher socio-economic backgrounds and have long-established academic traditions. All these factors have been proven to have an effect on achievement, with prior ability emerging as by far the most powerful predictor of examination success.

The next section of this report reviews the research literature since the publication of Bone's work about the achievements of boys and girls in single-sex and mixed schools. Since the EOC report in 1983 advances have been made in the analysis of school- and pupil-level data which has helped researchers control for background factors such as whether the school is single-sex or not. This enables then to compare like with like. The results of these studies have provided more sophisticated findings in relation to this debate which have enabled us to be more focused in our search for factors affecting the achievement of girls in girls-only and in mixed schools.

3
Academic Performance

PATTERNS OF EXAMINATION ENTRY AND PERFORMANCE AT 16

Since the introduction of the GCSE in 1988, more girls than boys have been entered for this examination. In 1997, for example, girls provided 51 per cent of the total GCSE entry; this figure has been maintained since 1988. The evidence of differences in boys' and girls' performance in the UK is usually drawn from the percentage A-C grades awarded in the GCSE (A*-C from 1994 onwards). While this may be an over-simplified approach and ignores the relative proportion of boys and girls not entered for the GCSE, it provides a widely understood yardstick and is used in the presentation of the statistics which follow.

In the GCSE, girls are gaining a higher proportion of the top grades (A*-C) than boys. The gap, in favour of girls, was 4 per cent in 1988 and has increased to 8 per cent in 1997. Both groups have been gaining more top grades generally, but the gap between the two genders has been growing steadily and shows no sign of decreasing. These statistics must, however, be interpreted in relation to the entry patterns. Even though more girls are entered for the GCSE, there are more boys amongst those classified as absent (those who enter but do not complete/ sit the examination) and those who do not enter at all. In 1997 53 per cent of all absentees were male. Also if we look at the core subjects of English and mathematics, an estimated 92 per cent of 16 year olds enter for GCSE English; 94 per cent of girls and 90 per cent of boys at this age. The comparative figures for mathematics are 95 per cent of 16 year olds entered; 98 per cent of girls and 95 per cent of boys at this age. These figures are not unimportant as such differences in entry policy must bear on the interpretation of the data, particularly if they represent lower attaining boys not being entered while girls with similar performance levels are.

Table 3.1 (on page 12) presents the entry and result figures for 12 major subjects taken at GCSE in 1997. What these figures show is that in only one of these subjects (biology) are boys substantially ahead of girls, a subject for which girls have traditionally entered in large numbers to meet the requirement of taking a science subject. In all the other 11 subjects girls are either substantially ahead of boys in the proportion of A*-C grades obtained or else the gap between the two groups is small. The two compulsory subjects of English and mathematics provide interesting result patterns considering that these subjects are compulsory for boys and girls at 16. The gender-related differences in English are substantial and have been increasing since 1988. Girls are now obtaining 16 per cent more A*-C grades than boys; a gap that has increased since 1988. In mathematics, the gap in performance is closing between the two groups and has been narrowing since 1988 to the extent that boys are now only 0.1 per cent ahead.

Table 3.1: Percentage of male/female entry and grades A*-C (all GCSE groups)

MAIN GCSE SUBJECTS 1997					
SUBJECT	% Entry Male (M)	% Entry Female (F)	% A*-C (M)	% A*-C (F)	Difference % A*-C (M-F)
Art/Design	48.4	51.6	52.9	70.8	−17.9
Biology	52.8	47.2	80.6	72.8	7.8
Chemistry	60.8	39.2	86.5	87.3	−0.8
Combined Science	49.6	50.4	47.7	49.1	−1.4
English	50.2	49.8	48.5	64.8	−16.3
English Literature	47.6	52.4	55.3	69.9	−14.6
French	46.5	53.5	43.9	57.7	−13.8
Geography	55.8	44.2	52.3	58.9	−6.6
History	48.7	51.3	54.6	61.7	−7.1
Maths	49.3	50.7	47.4	47.3	0.1
Technology	63.1	36.9	41.1	56.4	−15.3
Physics	63.1	36.9	86.5	85.8	0.7
ALL SUBJECTS	**49.3**	**50.7**	**50.3**	**58.7**	**−8.4**

M=male; F=female

(Source: 1997 Inter-Group Statistics, SEG, Surrey)

What seems to have been established in the result patterns of candidates taking the GCSE is that the examination system for 16 year olds is no longer failing girls, but that the main problem now is the under-achievement of boys at this stage. There is a widespread belief that through intervention strategies to attract girls into maths and science, girls' performance has increased and this concentration on girls as a focus group by teachers and researchers has been to the detriment of boys' performance. Such interventions have certainly broadened the styles of pedagogy and ways of working allowed in curriculum subjects, which has also been paralleled in the approach and style of the GCSE. These new approaches, however, especially in science, have concentrated on the learning of subjects in a wider, social context and have been found to increase both achievement and motivation for both boys and girls. Indeed results for both genders have been increasing over the years since the introduction of the GCSE.

PATTERNS OF EXAMINATION ENTRY AND PERFORMANCE AT 18

One of the main changes in A level examinations over the last 20 years is female entry patterns. More females enter for GCE A level; in 1997 they made up 53 per cent of the total entry having been only 39 per cent of the total entry in 1970. Table 3.2 shows the size of the effect of female entry patterns over the last 20 years. In most of the subjects examined at A level, the increase in candidature can be solely accounted for by the increase in the female entry.

What is becoming evident is that male/female entry patterns at A level are beginning to reflect those found at GCSE. This suggests, perhaps not surprisingly, that choices made at 16 are carried through to advanced level. However, evidence also shows large numbers of pupils wishing to opt out of subjects that had been compulsory at GCSE and show traditional patterns of entry in certain subjects when choice is introduced. For example, in mathematics, which is compulsory at 16, there are very different entry patterns emerging when choice is introduced. Almost 300,000 girls take GCSE maths, yet only 20,000 go on to take this subject at A Level. The opposite side of this coin is the

Table 3.2: Entry figures for eight major A level subjects by gender 1970-95

SUBJECT	SEX	1970	1980	1990	1995	% Diff 1970-1980	% Diff 1980-1990	% Diff 1990-1995
Biology	M	10,235	17,232	17,938	20,711	68.4	4.1	15.5
	F	9,463	20,662	28,517	31,553	118.3	38.0	10.6
	T	19,698	37,894	46,455	52,264	92.4	22.6	12.5
Chemistry	M	23,385	24,836	27,427	23,769	6.2	10.4	-13.3
	F	7,385	12,408	18,769	18,523	68.0	51.3	-1.3
	T	30,770	37,244	46,196	42,292	21.0	24.0	-8.5
English Literature	M	21,257	20,229	14,621	17,730	-4.8	-27.7	21.3
	F	34,736	45,371	32,345	40,444	30.6	-28.7	24.0
	T	55,993	65,600	46,966	58,174	17.2	-28.4	23.9
French	M	9,822	7,456	7,445	8,169	-24.1	-0.1	9.7
	F	16,103	18,640	19,799	19,394	15.8	6.2	-2.0
	T	25,925	26,096	27,244	27,563	0.7	4.4	1.2
Geography	M	19,421	20,714	23,524	23,887	6.7	13.6	1.5
	F	12,347	14,360	18,146	19,567	16.3	26.4	7.8
	T	31,768	35,074	41,670	43,454	10.4	18.8	4.3
History	M	18,145	18,898	19,845	19,490	4.1	5.0	-1.8
	F	16,811	21,196	23,962	24,306	26.1	13.0	1.4
	T	34,956	40,094	43,807	43,796	14.7	9.3	0.0
Maths	T	52,364	50,238	47,096	41,199	-4.1	-6.3	-12.5
	F	12,017	15,775	23,867	22,281	31.3	51.3	-6.6
	T	64,381	66,013	70,963	63,480	2.5	7.5	-10.5
Physics	M	35,045	35,752	35,300	27,231	2.0	-1.3	-22.9
	F	6,501	9,406	10,029	7,571	44.7	6.6	-24.5
	T	41,546	45,158	45,329	34,802	8.7	0.4	-23.2
TOTAL ALL ABOVE SUBJECTS	**M**	**189,674**	**195,355**	**193,196**	**182,186**	**3.0**	**-1.1**	**-5.7**
	F	**115,363**	**157,818**	**175,434**	**183,639**	**36.8**	**11.2**	**4.7**
	T	**305,037**	**353,173**	**368,630**	**365,825**	**15.8**	**4.4**	**-0.7**

Source: University of Oxford Delagacy of Local Examinations Archive, Willmot 1994;
Inter-Board Statistics 1990, 1995, Associated Examining Board.

male entry in English literature which shows only 17,000 males going on to study A level English literature when 200,000 had studied the subject at GCSE. Again it is important to consider these entry populations when we review performance patterns.

Over the eight-year period (1990-97) the gap in performance between boys and girls, grades A-C at A level, has been decreasing steadily. The gap in favour of boys in 1990 was 2.8 per cent grades A-C. In 1997 girls were shown to be 1.2 per cent A-C grades ahead of boys. However, the A-C benchmark hides more striking patterns at each of the separate grades and a closer look at certain subjects identifies a 'cross-over' that takes place in male/female result patterns between GCSE and A level.

Table 3.3: Differences in % A-C Grades in A level Examinations 1991-97

SUBJECT	MALE—FEMALE (M-F) DIFFERENCE IN % A-C GRADES ALL GCE GROUPS				MEAN DIFFERENCE
	1991	1993	1995	1997	1991–97
Biology	1.8	0.5	−2.0	−3.5	−0.8
Chemistry	1.3	1.5	0.7	−2.5	0.3
Physics	1.0	−0.9	−1.5	−4.3	−1.4
Mathematics	1.2	−0.4	−2.3	−2.5	−1.0
French	3.5	4.6	4.1	0.9	3.3
English Lit	3.5	1.9	1.2	0.6	1.8
Geography	−3.6	−2.9	−4.9	−7.6	−4.8
History	5.0	3.2	1.8	2.5	3.1
TOTAL ALL SUBJECTS	**2.3**	**0.9**	**−0.3**	**−1.2**	**0.4**

Source: Inter-Board Statistics 1991-97, AEB Guildford

Table 3.3 shows the male/female differences in the percentage of A–C grades obtained in eight A level subjects. From the last column headed 'mean difference' in Table 3.3 it can be seen that there is a cross-over in the patterns of performance at A level, which shows that the gaps between male and female performance are much smaller and less consistent at the higher grades at A level. The impressive results obtained by girls at 16 are not replicated in examinations at 18. These gender differences in performance are also influenced by the populations who sit these examinations at A level. Very traditional entry patterns still exist post-16, alongside small groups of very selective, able students entering for subjects that are less traditional in relation to their gender. These small, selective groups usually do better than the larger more 'mixed ability' group. Examples of these groups would be boys taking English literature and females taking physics.

The purpose of this statistical review has been to establish that there are different take-up and outcomes by gender between the GCSE and A level and that a cross-over in result patterns emerge between the two stages of examining. Other recent research has shown that these patterns found at A level are maintained well into higher education where there is concern about the differential gap in performance amongst males and females in the higher classifications of degree (Gender Working Party Report, 1994). This section has highlighted the very complex nature of the patterns of performance with which we are presented.

There have been very few research studies that considered the interaction of gender with social class and race when looking at achievement in school. All these three variables are of importance when considering pupils' achievements in public examinations. Gillborn and Gipps (1996) cite a study based on the Youth Cohort Study (YCS) that offers information on the interaction of all three of these variables. Table 3.4 summarises the results of this project, showing the average exam performance scores for pupils arranged by social class (professional, intermediate and manual), ethnic background (African Caribbean, Asian, white) and gender.

Table 3.4: Average examination scores by social class, ethnic origin and gender (1985)

ETHNIC AND SOCIAL CLASS GROUP		AVERAGE EXAMINATION SCORE		NUMBER OF CASES
		MALE	FEMALE	
AFRICAN CARIBBEAN	Professional	27.1	24.9	12
	Intermediate	21.1	18.1	68
	Manual	14.3	15.6	115
ASIAN	Professional	30.7	27.8	17
	Intermediate	27.2	25.9	95
	Manual	23.3	22.5	189
WHITE	Professional	30.4	32.3	2,118
	Intermediate	23.7	25.6	3,903
	Manual	17.6	20.6	5,218

Source: Gillborn and Gipps, 1996:16

Table 3.4 shows that social class is strongly associated with achievement regardless of gender and ethnic background. Whatever a pupil's gender or ethnic origin, those from higher social class backgrounds do better on average. The data suggests that the relationship between gender and achievement is not as simple as perhaps thought. In this case, the patterns of girls outperforming boys was only uniformly true of white pupils, it was not true of Asian pupils in any social class and only applied to African Caribbean pupils from manual backgrounds. There is no data which looks at these three variables and also performance in single-sex schools. It would be of considerable interest to know how the interaction of gender, race and class affects performance in single-sex schools as well as coeducational schools. It would be of interest to know the differential effectiveness of single-sex schools for different sub-groups.

PATTERNS OF PERFORMANCE IN SINGLE-SEX AND COEDUCATIONAL SCHOOLS

The EOC/Ofsted review of performance differences of boys and girls at school (EOC/Ofsted, 1996) argues that in 'almost all the areas covered by the Framework for Inspection, girls' schools are generally found to perform best' (p.24). They also go on to acknowledge that there are marked variations in the position of individual schools, both single-sex and mixed-sex, within the hierarchy of schools and that much depends on the socio-economic context of the school and the ability profile of its intake. The background factors of the schools and those of the pupils are of crucial importance when trying to identify whether a certain type of school is better for one group over another. This is one of the most consistent findings across all the research studies carried out in this field of inquiry; when attempts have been made to control statistically for differences in ability and social class of intakes, the apparent discrepancy in examination performance between coeducational and single-sex schools largely disappears (Arnot et al, 1998; Bone, 1983; Daly, 1996; Hannan et al, 1996; ILEA, 1990a, b; Nuttall et al, 1992; Rowe, 1988; Sammons, 1995; Steedman, 1984, 1985; Thomas et al, 1993; Thomas et al, 1994; Thomas and Elliot, 1996,1997).

The following sections review the research cited above, that has looked specifically at whether girls do better in single-sex schools

Daly (1996) reviews much of the literature related to research findings concerning the impact of different types of secondary school organization on girls' achievement. He suggests that much of the research in this area reflects the scarcity of studies with adequate controls for pre-existing differences. He acknowledges that while there are still technical difficulties surrounding researchers' attempts to deal with non-equivalent groups, the wider availability of new computer software for the multilevel modelling of nested data enables better estimates to be made in relation to the achievements of different groups from different school types.

The Inner London Education Authority (ILEA) monitored single-sex and mixed-sex school performance differences through out the 1980s as part of its equal opportunities policies. Daly (op. cit.) reports that the ILEA analysis of pupil data for 1980 indicated that little difference in overall public examination achievement for 15 and 16 year olds was related to attendance at single-sex or mixed schools. This study controlled for prior ability which was measured by performance in verbal and non-verbal ability tests. Later analyses showed contradictory results. The 1983 data analysis did not support the earlier 1980 analysis. The 1983 data showed girls in single-sex schools having significantly higher overall achievement than girls in mixed schools after controlling for prior ability (ILEA, 1990a). Results for 1987, however, indicated that the achievement differences for girls were not significantly related to single-sex/mixed-sex school differences after adjustments for intake differences. The reasons for the varying results were considered to be related to the more widespread implementation of equal opportunity policies in schools within the authority, but perhaps more importantly to the use of new statistical procedures that provided more reliable estimates for the 1987 data (ILEA, 1990b).

More recent studies in this area have been based on the multilevel analysis of data. Again the findings are not conclusive, but this statistical technique of looking at data at both the pupil and school level has provided more reliable results than previous research studies in this field. Nuttall et al. (1992) investigated patterns of examination performance of 15 and 16 year old pupils from 42 schools in four local educational authorities. This study was carried out for the Association of Metropolitan Authorities (AMA). In their analysis they were able to control for pupil-level data, such as gender, verbal reasoning band, ethnicity and eligibility for free school meals which stands as an approximate measure of social class or poverty. They were also able to control for a variety of school-level factors as well, such as management (church/state) and status (comprehensive, selective, independent, etc.).

From their analysis, Nuttall et al. showed that differences between school gender (i.e. single-sex or mixed sex) were not significant. These investigations were repeated in 1993 and 1994 (Thomas et al., 1993; Thomas et al., 1994). In the 1993 study, 116 schools from nine local authorities were involved. After similar adjustments for pupil and school level factors, girls were found to perform significantly better at single-sex schools. However, the 1994 study, which involved 87 schools from seven local authorities, reported no significant differences between the performance of girls at single-sex and coeducational schools. The researchers themselves note the problems with methodology in using this type of analysis and the limitations of school-level data. However, they do suggest that the 1994 results are more accurate then those of 1993 due to better integration of missing data and better development of the software used to analyse the data.

Daly (1996) looked at the effects of single-sex and coeducational secondary schooling on girls' achievement in Northern Ireland. Unlike most of England and Wales, Northern Ireland has an academically selective secondary school system and education is also characterised by a strong partnership between church and state in the provision of single-sex schooling. Many of the single-sex schools, therefore, are connected to either the catholic or protestant churches. Single-sex schooling is such an integral part of the education system in the area, that any move towards coeducation has been treated cautiously to the extent that 'public perceptions of the superior academic effectiveness of single-sex schools are a matter of considerable importance to policy makers in the light of any "trend" towards coeducation' (Daly, 1996:295).

It is also of interest, perhaps, that many of those secondary schools that are mixed-sex are integrated, non-religious schools.

Daly's (1996) own study as based on the reanalysis of public examination data for pupils at 16, at pupil and school levels. His findings, he suggests, are broadly in line with many other studies of a similar type in Northern Ireland, England, USA and Australia (Gallagher et al, 1996; Steedman, 1985; Marsh, 1989; Gill, 1993). In conclusion, he reports that the data from Northern Ireland add further support to the view that 'after due allowance for pre-existing differences, the academic advantages of single-sex schooling for girls are far from conclusive at this stage. Significant interactions, of substantive importance, were not found in this analysis of girls' achievement' (Daly 1996:301).

Smithers and Robinson (1995) looked in detail at the performance of boys and girls in single-sex schools from both the state and independent sectors. When the researchers were able to compare like with like, they found that the differences between coeducational and single-sex schools largely disappeared. In measuring the effectiveness of different school types, Smithers and Robinson cited work by Sammons et al (1994) that argued that about 30 per cent of the variation of exam results can be explained by ability of intake, 6 per cent by social and cultural background and 9 per cent by school effects. The main findings of the Sammons et al (1994) study, as summarized by Smithers and Robinson, are shown in Table 3.5. Smithers and Robinson concluded that the outstanding results of girls in girls-only schools and boys in boys-only schools at GCSE and A level were not due to single-sexness alone, but rather to factors associated with it such as ability, social class, history and tradition.

In their latest report (*Coeducation and Single-Sex Schools – Revisited,* 1997), Smithers and Robinson present a re-analysis of the 1995 GCSE results for English schools carried out by the DfEE. From this analysis the researchers have been able to compare the performance of girls from girls' schools with girls in coeducational schools and boys in boys'

Table 3.5: School Effectiveness

	MEASURES	% GCSE PERFORMANCE
SECONDARY	Prior Attainment	30.6
	Socio-Cultural Factors	6.0
	School Effects	8.8
PRIMARY	Reading and Maths Scores (Age 7)	22.8
	Verbal Reasoning and Reading (Age 11)	6.0
	Socio-Cultural Factors	8.4
	School Effects	4.2

Source: Sammons et al (1994) in Smithers and Robinson (1995:3).

schools with boys in coeducational schools across different school types. The researchers report that these data further illustrate how difficult it is to uncover the real effects of types of school. Table 3.6 below shows the data re-analysed by Smithers and Robinson from their 1997 report.

Table 3.6: GCSE Results 1995 – % of boys and girls with 5+ A*-C grades (N)

	SCHOOL TYPE	IND (44,196)	SEL (8,727)	GM (92,697)	COMP (379,739)	OTHER (16,948)	TOTAL (542,307)
GIRLS	Single-sex (44,558)	91.3	96.9	71.3	45.5	35.8	68.9
	Co-ed (222,756)	81.3	91.1	50.8	45.4	25.9	47.2
BOYS	Single-sex (36,095)	89.7	95.5	65.2	33.9	18.5	63.5
	Co-ed (238,754)	79.0	89.4	41.0	36.2	18.1	38.8
	TOTAL (542,307)	**85.9**	**94.8**	**50.2**	**40.7**	**23.2**	**46.4**

Source: Smithers and Robinson, 1997:3.

The data presented in Table 3.6 above shows that pupils in single-sex schools do seem to do better than those in coeducational schools, but that more of the single-sex schools would be those independent and grammar schools with high ability intakes. As can be seen from Table 3.6, many of the apparent differences disappear when school types are considered separately. For example, girls from coeducational comprehensives do just as well as their counterparts in single-sex schools. It is also interesting to note that the difference between selective boys' schools and selective girls' schools is quite small. However, some of the largest differences are between girls and boys attending the same type of school. This reflects the national picture of girls doing better than boys generally at GCSE. In further analysis of comprehensive school data from Ofsted, Smithers and Robinson show that differences between comprehensive schools is greater in relation to the presence of a sixth form or not than whether the school is single-sex or not.

They further go on to review the 1997 GCSE results from different types of independent school (whether day or boarding, whether selective or non-selective). They show that girls in fully coeducational schools in the independent sector perform as well as, if not better than, their counterparts in single-sex independent schools. In selective, coeducational day schools, girls obtained 95.4 per cent 5+ A*-C grades at GCSE, whereas 94.3 per cent of girls in selective, single-sex, day schools did likewise. In this analysis of independent schools, boys in selective, boys-only, day schools performed as well as girls in similar schools, with 95.1 per cent obtaining 5+ A*-C grades at GCSE. This group also go on to perform the best overall at A level. At 18+ they are ahead over all other school types including the corresponding girls' schools.

In conclusion, Smithers and Robinson (1997) argue that while the findings presented in their report cannot be regarded as conclusive, they can, however, be sure that there is not a single-sex effect on all occasions. The argument stated 15 years ago by Bone (1983) that single-sex schools do better than their coeducational counterparts not because they separate the sexes, but because of other factors, is reinforced:

> the pattern of differences and similarities strongly suggests that the performance of a school in terms of examination results has much less to do with whether it is single-sex or not than with other factors.
> (Smithers and Robinson, 1997:5)

Daly (1996) reminds us however, that it is important to stress that academic achievement is only one of the goals pursued in schools, although an important one. Policy-makers, employers, higher education gatekeepers, parents and teachers and pupils themselves may differ about the extent of its importance. Academic achievement is only one aspect of a complex debate about single-sex schooling. Section 5 of this report will look at some factors other than achievement that indicate why single-sex schooling may still be desirable and beneficial for some girls. The next section (Section 4), however will stay with the theme of academic achievement from an international perspective.

4
Academic performance from an international perspective

Many of the findings from research carried out in England, Wales and Northern Ireland have been supported from research studies in other countries. The following sections of this report review those findings which have come mainly from the developed world. Very few studies exist from less developed countries or education systems. Also the developing nations would have particular problems in relation to the issues under investigation, especially as not all children in developing nations have the same amount, or indeed similar experiences, of education. Studies from the USA, Australia and Ireland are reviewed below as examples of work in the girls and girls-only schooling debate from an international perspective.

AUSTRALIA

Daly (1996) suggests that not a great deal of recent Australian research has been directly concerned with estimating the relative effectiveness of single-sex and coeducational schooling in terms of academic outcomes. Gill (1993) reviewed the Australian research literature on single-sex versus coeducational schooling. She reports that the situation in Australia is very similar to that in the UK with some educators taking up highly publicized positions in favour of single-sex education for girls, with others arguing strongly in favour of coeducation. Gill (1993) also acknowledges the challenges that researchers face in disentangling school effects from other related effects. From a large-scale study of these issues in Queensland (Carpenter, 1985), the findings echo those of Bone (1983) in that the researcher wrote of the multiplicity of confounding variables and that school gender context, by itself, did not account for significant variations in student outcomes (Gill, 1993).

In the early 1990s, the number of single-sex schools in Australia was declining sharply in both the public and private sectors and had been doing so since the early 1970s. Gill suggest that the most obvious reasons for this decline were economic pressures rather than educational theories. Her conclusions about the Australian research that has been conducted in the area of single-sex versus coeducational schooling, are that it has not been possible to present conclusive findings on the relative merits of single-sex and coeducation from the perspective of optimal education for girls.

In line with these observations, Yates (1993), in an overview of girls education in Australia, suggested that overall, research on achievement effects had established no clear superiority of either coeducation or single-sex schooling for girls once other factors are controlled for.

USA

Of those schools in the USA which continued to offer some form of single-sex provision, the majority of them were catholic secondary schools. Riordan (1985) conducted a major research project which looked at catholic single-sex and coeducation schools compared with public coeducation schools using a representative sample of high school seniors. After controlling for socio-economic status, he found that girls from single-sex schools had superior verbal test scores but not mathematics scores. However, Riordan acknowledged that without information on prior ability or attainment, the findings could not be regarded as school effects (Daly 1996). Riordan went on to review the research literature in the USA in this area and concluded that more comprehensive data and improved techniques of analysis were needed before any firm conclusions could be drawn about the effects of single-sex schools on achievement.

The work of Lee and Bryk (1986) which analysed the effects of single-sex schooling based on catholic schools' data from the 'High School and Beyond' Survey, claimed that students, especially female students, benefited academically and attitudinally from single-sex schooling. However, these findings were later challenged by Marsh (1989) using the same data. Marsh claimed that there was insufficient evidence of school-type differences in attainment because of limited controls for pre-existing differences in the original study. Marsh argued that the attainment differences between pupils in single-sex and coeducational catholic schools were not significant after adequate adjustment for the intakes.

IRELAND

The most recent study to investigate the issues of single-sex and coeducational schooling in Ireland is that carried out by Hannan et al. (1996) that used a multilevel modelling approach in analyzing the data.

The findings from the Hanna et al. (1996) study found that coeducational and single-sex schools in Ireland differ in a number of respects, many of which parallel those factors associated with these types of schools in the UK. First, single-sex schools tend to be more selective in their intake than coeducation schools which results in a very different social and ability profile of pupils in the two school types. Second, coeducation schools are more likely to allocate pupils to classes on the basis of their academic ability ('streaming' or 'banding') and third, coeducational and single-sex schools differ in the type of curriculum taught and the way in which subjects and levels are made available to classes and pupils. Hannan et al. suggest that these differences are related not to education as such but rather to the historical origins of the secondary, vocational and community/comprehensive sectors of schooling: coeducational secondary schools resemble more closely single-sex secondary schools than they do other coeducational schools in the vocational and community sectors.

In comparing like with like by controlling for these background factors, the Hannan et al. study found that at 16, coeducation had a slight negative effect on girls' overall examination performance in the Junior Certificate: girls in single-sex schools were at a slight advantage compared to girls in coeducational schools, though girls in mixed-sex schools did better than boys in these schools. However, this effect of coeducation was 'substantively very small' (Hannan et al., 1996:196). In fact, most of the difference in performance between coeducational and single-sex schools was due to differences in the social background and ability of their pupil intakes. Interestingly, however, Hannan et al (1996) showed that the impact of coeducation was strongest amongst pupils of below-average academic ability. Among lower-ability pupils, boys in coeducational schools do slightly better and girls in coeducational schools slightly worse, than their counterparts in single-sex schools. This is compared with examination performance of middle- and higher-ability pupils where being in a coeducational school has little substantive impact on examination performance.

In examination performance at 18 (the Leaving Certificate), being in a coeducational school has no significant impact on boys' and girls' results when social background, prior performance and other schooling factors are controlled for. Schools differ significantly from one another in average performance but again, this is 'primarily because of the type of pupils attending them, and the way in which pupils are allocated to classes, not whether they are coeducational or single-sex' (Hannan et al., 1996:197).

DEVELOPING COUNTRIES

There is very little evidence of the effect of single-sex or coeducational schooling on achievement of boys and girls in developing countries. Daly (1996) gives a brief summary of some of the research studies that have been carried out. He suggests that two recent studies have provided qualified support for the superiority of single-sex schooling for girls. Jiminez and Lockheed's (1989) study of the mathematics attainment of eighth graders in Thailand suggested the superiority of single-sex schooling for girls. However, these researchers did acknowledge that most single-sex schools in Thailand were private schools while most mixed-sex schools were public schools and that there was also great variation within school type.

Another study of mathematics achievement of senior pupils from Nigeria in public-sector schools also suggested that girls achieved more at single-sex than at mixed-sex schools (Lee and Lockheed, 1990). However, as Daly (1996) warns us we must review the findings of studies from developing countries with caution as comparisons of schooling within countries that are at different stages of development are difficult to interpret.

SUMMARY

In summary, therefore, it would seem that most of the studies which have investigated the differential impact of single-sex and mixed-sex schooling in other countries have produced similar findings to those from studies conducted within the UK. While the majority of the studies reviewed have produced at some stage evidence that suggests that girls attending single-sex institutions do better in examination performance, the data is by no means conclusive. Indeed, it is reiterated that what accounts for girls doing better in these schools is not that they are single-sex per se but because of the ability and social background of the intake and the histories and traditions of the schools.

A study by Baker et al. (1995) suggests that the effect of single-sex schooling on academic achievement may be enhanced or decreased by the context in which single-sex schooling is used within a country's system of schooling. For example, if a country has a balance of single-sex and coeducational schools, the effect of single-sex schooling is less pronounced compared to the effect within a country that has very little single-sex schooling which is associated with particular (commonly elite) groups of students.

The work by Hannan et al. (1996) interestingly identified that some schools might be better for particular sub-groups of pupils, such as lower ability students. Many of the differences among pupils in educational performance are primarily related to individual differences in academic ability and social background. Pupils from lower socio-economic backgrounds continue to be at a disadvantage generally within the schooling system, irrespective of whether the school is single-sex or not. More research both at a national and international level on how effective different schools are for different sub-groups within categories (for example, low-ability working-class girls) would be extremely helpful in clarifying some of the issues further.

5
School and Social Factors

EDUCATIONAL EXPERIENCE

There is evidence within the research literature that suggests that the everyday experience of girls and boys in school is very different (Leonard, 1996). Many of the proponents of single-sex schooling argue that girls' experience of schooling in single-sex schools is far better than that of girls who attend coeducational schools and that girls' self-esteem and their critical self-awareness is better in single-sex situations (Deem, 1984; Mahony, 1985). Researchers have puzzled over the drop in girls' self-esteem as they go through school even though they do as well as, or even better than, boys in many examinations and assessments

(AAUW, 1992). The AAUW report, *How Schools Short Change Girls*, attributes this drop in self-esteem to the negative messages delivered to girls by school curricula. The authors acknowledge that there has been no social science research to document cause and effect in this matter, but that schools must take more responsibility for understanding that the curriculum 'is the central message-giving instrument of the school' (AAUW, 1992:67).

Gill (1993) compared the cognitive self-esteem of girls in coeducational classes with that of boys and that of girls in girls-only classes. Students were asked to rank themselves in relation to the rest of their class. The majority of boys assigned themselves a rank in the top half of the class in direct contrast to their female classmates, the majority of whom assigned themselves to the bottom half of the class. In the single-sex group an equally high proportion of the girls put themselves in the top half of the class. When students' self rankings were checked against teachers' perceptions it was immediately evident that in the mixed classrooms, even when the teachers identified girls as the top students, the girls themselves seemed unaware of this, while the boys were sure of their position. In the all girls' classrooms, the group who were nominated by the teacher as the top group accurately rated themselves in this position. This effect was independent of whether or not the teacher was male or female. Gill argues that what is suggested by this result is that the processes of the mixed classrooms work to affirm boys' understanding of their own merit at the same time as undermining that of the girls, whereas in all girls' classrooms, the negative references group does not occur and girls can get a clearer picture of their own ability.

In her extensive report for the EOC, Bone (1983) suggested that up until 1983 the research showed that girls in girls-only schools did not have to compete with boys for the attention of their teachers, they did not find their abilities mocked by boys and were less afraid to speak out in class. However, for girls themselves, they did not see girls-only schools as the main solutions to these problems. They did seem to favour, however, the introduction of single-sex classes for certain subjects (see section 5.6). Observations in mixed schools also revealed that teachers of both sexes tended to treat girls and boys in the same classrooms differently, in a way that forces girls into a passive role. There was no evidence that the teaching style of women teachers were particularly well-matched to the learning styles of girls. There were indications however, that both girls and boys concentrated more on the task in hand with a teacher of the same sex.

Much of the research literature that promotes the advantages of single-sex schools for girls discusses negative aspects of the social interactions between girls and boys in mixed-sex schools. For example, Mahony (1985) in her study of the interaction of boys and girls in three co-educational London comprehensive schools, found many examples of sexual harassment of girls by boys and the marked dominance of boys in the class. She argued that an enormous amount of time and energy is expended by boys in what amounts in the end to the social control of girls. Proponents of single-sex schooling argue that girls-only schools offer a space for girls in which to learn and achieve without undue harassment and interference from boys (Deem, 1984; Leonard, 1996; Mahony, 1985). However, other research has shown that girls-only and boys-only environments create their own social interactions, not all of which are positive (Smithers and Robinson, 1997).

ATTITUDES TO SCHOOL

Research that has investigated pupils' attitudes to schooling has shown a general shift in positive and negative attitudes expressed by boys and girls towards their schooling experiences in general and to learning in different subjects in particular (e.g. Barber, 1994; Gallagher et al., 1996; Rudduck et al., 1996; Stables and Stables, 1995). These studies tend to suggest that girls are now more positive about school than boys, are more likely to enjoy school than boys, and by the end of primary schooling are more likely to conform to the norms of schooling and work harder. Harris, Nixon, and Rudduck (1993) suggest that girls do better in school because they learn to work within the conventions of school which tend to emphasize neat presentation, attention to learning within the classroom and social interactions around the school.

Boys, on the other hand tend to conform less to the social norms of school, pay less attention to the neatness and presentation of their work and consistently tend to overrate their ability (Barber, 1994). Boys also tend to be more selective in terms of the subjects which they see has having value and in which they will work hard (Stobart et al., 1992). Boys' disaffection with school in comparison to girls' resides particularly in the area of motivation to learn (Barber, op. cit.). By their mid teens, girls were consistently more motivated than boys. Evidence from interviews with students (Barber, op. cit.) indicates that it is not 'cool' for boys of that age to be seen by their peers as 'achievers'.

Can attitudes to school, learning and pupils' own self-development be attributed to boys and girls generally or are they different for boys and girls in coeducation and single-sex schools? The research work of Hannan et al (1996) shows that pupils in coeducational schools have a more positive view of their schools' impact on their social and personal development than pupils in single-sex schools. However, 15 to 16-year-old boys in co-educational schools tend to have somewhat lower academic self-images, lower senses of control and are more critical of their appearance than their counterparts in single-sex schools. Thus being in a coeducational school seems to make boys more self-critical. Hannan et al (op. cit.) also show that coeducation has some effect on gender-role expectations. In particular, 18-year-old boys tend to have less traditional views of work and family roles when they attend coeducational schools.

The same positive effects on gender-role expectations were not found amongst girls attending coeducational schools at a similar age. In fact, girls have less confidence and lower senses of control than boys no matter what school they attend. In measures of personal and social development, Hannan et al. (1996) found that even given their higher levels of achievement, girls are less confident about their academic abilities, do not feel the same sense of control over their lives, and are more critical of their appearance than boys with similar backgrounds and schooling experiences. In addition girls are still subject to traditional gender stereotyping and carry a heavier domestic workload than boys irrespective of what school they attend. It is acknowledged that the Hannan et al. (1996) study is related to the Irish social and economic context in which it was conducted. However, even within this context the findings are of importance given people's perceptions about the recent success of girls at school and the opportunities this creates for them for further and higher education and beyond.

PUPILS' VIEWS OF SINGLE-SEX AND COEDUCATIONAL SCHOOLING

Smithers and Robinson (1997) were interested in the views of students who had experiences of attending either single-sex or coeducational schools. As part of a wider study, they interviewed 100 students in their first year at a high-ranking university about these issues. The sample of students were balanced in terms of attendance at single-sex/ coeducational school, girls/boys and independent/state schools. Students were asked to comment on their experiences of school and to rate whether they felt that their school was better for them academically or socially. The results of these ratings are shown in Table 5.1. In the first instance the data reflected the common perception that single-sex schools are experienced as more beneficial academically and co-educational schools more beneficial socially. However, as Smithers and Robinson report, closer inspection of the data reveals a more complex pattern of ratings that 'further underlies the difficulty of making comparisons between schools on just one dimension when they differ on so many' (1997:7).

Table 5.1: Students' favourable ratings of their schools[1] (N)

		ACADEMICALLY	SOCIALLY
GIRLS[2]	Single-sex	73.6 (19)	50.0 (16)
	Coeducational	42.1 (19)	87.5 (16)
BOYS[3]	Single-sex	72.2 (18)	64.3 (14)
	Coeducational	63.2 (19)	78.9 (19)
[1] Does not include those with experience of both			
[2] Difference for girls statistically significant – academically and socially			
[3] No statistical differences for boys			

Source: Smithers and Robinson, 1997:7.

When independent and state schools were separated in the analysis, the data showed that coeducational independent schools were rated as favourably in academic terms as their single-sex counterparts. There was a difference between the ratings relating to the academic benefit of state schools by students who went to coeducational state schools and those who went single-sex state schools. Smithers and Robinson suggest that this difference is consistent with what we already know about differences between the comprehensives which are usually the coeducational state schools and the grammars which are usually the single-sex state schools. Both boys and girls from coeducational state schools rated their schools as more beneficial from a social perspective than an academic one. Girls from single-sex state schools rated their schools as more beneficial academically than socially, whereas boys from single-sex state schools thought that their schools were balanced between their social and academic benefits.

Smithers and Robinson go on to conclude that girls who had attended single-sex schools tended to fear there might have been distractions had there been boys present, seemed to value having been pushed academically, yet voiced reservations about single-sex environments for girls being too competitive, and prone to spitefulness. In contrast to this, girls who had attended coeducational schools regarded teaching the sexes together as the natural thing to do and rejected the idea that boys had dominated the lessons in their schools. They also agreed that it was better to have both male and female perspectives when studying in the sixth form, and that their experience of coeducational schooling had made it easier in adjusting to life in higher education.

Boys, on the other hand, were less vociferous about differences between single-sex and coeducation. Boys from both these types of school tended to agree that there was no difference socially between the two types of schools and that academically there was little difference. If any difference did occur it was between state and independent schools. Boys generally felt that it was better to be educated with girls, as this helped in general social adjustment and moving into mixed-sex situations at university.

Of those students who had experiences both types of schools (mainly by moving at the sixth form stage) it was interesting to note that more girls moved to coeducational or boys' schools with sixth forms attached whereas most boys found their schools becoming mixed-sex around them. There is little research to date which has investigated the impact of such organisational changes on pupils and how pupils themselves cope in these situations.

SUBJECT CHOICE

The academic disadvantage of coeducation has not only been reported in the literature in terms of examination performance but also through differences in subject choice. The tendency for subject choice to become polarized is well known (Burgess, 1990) and affects boys as well as girls.

When educated together, girls and boys feel the need to assert their sexual identity and define themselves by means of behaviour and subject choice. Thus subjects acquire a masculine/feminine connotation which, in effect, restricts the individuals' freedom of choice. Pupils who choose to counteract these gender stereotypes often come up against problems that are not necessarily related to the subject itself but that have more to do with imbalances between the sexes in the classroom and how boys, girls and teachers work and co-operate in these situations

In earlier studies there was concern that single-sex girls' schools did not provide, as a matter of course, the range of subjects that were nominally available to girls in coeducational schools. Bone (1983) suggested that up until the early 1980s, girls' schools as a whole did not provide the facilities to make 'male' subjects more available to girls as they were in mixed schools. Neither, with the possible exception of girls' grammars, did girls-only schools make use of the mechanisms of compulsory subjects or option schemes to encourage girls to depart from stereotype. However, Bone (1983) suggests that girls themselves tended to choose areas of study more associated with boys when they were in girls-only schools and that the interests of girls and boys were closer together in the single-sex sector than in coeducational schools. In relation to actual choice, however, the courses girls took and the examinations that they entered were just as determined by gender in girls-only schools as in mixed schools although there did seem to be more girls taking science in girls-only grammar schools.

Bone (1983) suggests that choice of subject has to be seen as a product of differing influences, and not just gendered choices. Pupils in high academic schools (mostly single-sex) were protected from the most marked source of stereotyping detected in subject choice as between girls' schools and mixed schools. Vocational subjects were more generally provided and taken up by pupils in mixed schools. The entry for vocational subjects at this time was highly differentiated by sex and the vocational subjects themselves tended to be geared towards separate male and female roles in the workplace. Vocational subjects also provided the possibility for certain students, particularly lower ability students, to avoid the less popular male and female ends of the traditional academic curriculum. Vocational qualifications in the 1990s are quite different from their predecessors in the early 1980s and many more schools are offering general vocational qualifications to their students. However, the patterns of entry in these new vocational qualifications are still highly differentiated by sex and decisions about up-take are still very much influenced by future work aspirations (Felstead, 1998).

Both Stables (1990) and Colley et al. (1994) have looked at the differences of pupils' subject preferences, their enjoyment of, and attitudes to, school in relation to the type of school they attend (whether single-sex or coeducational). These studies were conducted in a different climate to that of Bone's (1983) with schools having to work within a new national curriculum which (a) limited the choice that had previously been available to pupils at 14 years and (b) legislated for the teaching and testing of the core subjects of English, science and mathematics at Key Stage 3(14) and Key Stage 4 (16). Therefore, subjects which both genders may have avoided in previous years were now compulsory.[1]

Stables (1990) compared the attitudes of 13 and 14 year-old pupils from single sex and co-educational comprehensive schools towards school subjects, and particular science subjects. His results showed that generally, boys' and girls' attitudes to curriculum subjects are more strongly polarized in mixed schools than in single-sex ones. With regard to subject preference, single-sex educated boys were much keener on drama, biology and languages than their mixed-sex counterparts who had a greater relative enjoyment of physics and physical sciences. Physics (overall the most 'masculine' subject in terms of difference in the subject preferences between the sexes) was better liked by girls in single-sex schools than by girls in mixed schools.

As far as the perception of subject importance was concerned, the type of school had little effect on the overall sex differences. Coeducated boys, however, were less convinced of the value of music and drama than were those from single-sex schools. Girls from single-sex schools considered drama and craft to be more important than their coeducated counterparts, as well as physics. Stables (1990) concludes by suggesting that the danger is that subject interest and specialization may be guided to a greater extent to conform to a received sexual stereotype in mixed schools than in single-sex schools. This has an effect on equal opportunities for girls (and boys) in mixed schools, as it effectively narrows their career choices.

In the work by Colley et al. (1994), preference for less stereotyped subjects by girls in single-sex schools was found to be connected with, and affected by, the age of pupils. Pupils of 11-12 years and 15-16 years from single-sex and coeducational state comprehensive schools were asked about their subject preferences. In the younger age group (11-12 years), girls from single-sex schools showed much stronger preferences for the 'male' stereotyped subjects of mathematics and science than girls from co-educational schools. The 'female' stereotyped subjects of music and art were higher in preference for boys from single-sex schools than for boys from coeducational schools, while the reverse was true of science. The preferences of the older pupils (15-16 years) show gender rather than school type differences.

Colley at al. (1994) suggest that one possible explanation of the age difference derives from a 'gender intensification' hypothesis. This hypothesis suggest that females adopt more rigid gender-related rules for behaviour at adolescence and predicts that greater gender-stereotyping of attitudes and behaviour will occur at and during adolescence in girls as adult gender roles are anticipated and enacted. It is therefore possible that attitudes towards school subjects become more gender stereotyped among female pupils as they progress through secondary school. The process of adopting and identifying adult gender roles may have overridden the effects of school type in the older group of pupils.

PARENTAL CHOICE AND THE ROLE OF GIRLS IN EDUCATION MARKETS

Parental Choice

One of the consequences of the market philosophy in education has been the ability of parents to have more control over their choice of secondary school for their sons and daughters. To date relatively little research has looked at parents' reasons for sending their children to either single-sex or coeducational schools.

Early work carried out by ILEA (1985) suggested that it was not possible to identify precisely the reasons behind parental choice of a single-sex school because single-sex schools in the local authority were associated with ex-grammar schools and 'good' academic reputations. The fact that some of the single-sex schools that had been formerly secondary modern schools were under-subscribed tended to promote the view that it is the overall reputation of the school itself that motivates parents to choose it rather than whether it is single-sex or not. However, the ILEA work did suggest that many parents of daughters, in particular, did subscribe to some of the views in favour of girls-only schools.

West and Hunter (1993) studied the views of parents of first-year pupils in 18 London secondary schools. The researchers were interested what these parents thought about mixed and single-sex schooling in general. West and Hunter found that the majority of their sample of parents who had sent their children to mixed-sex schools thought that there was no good reason to separate boys and girls at 11 after primary school and that mixed schools prepare children better for adult life. Very few parents thought that mixed schools were better for boys because of the 'civilizing' influence of girls, but they did feel that there were social advantages for boys and girls being educated together. Nor did many parents think that mixed schools were better for girls because they take equal opportunities issues more seriously or because girls' schools are less well equipped than mixed schools. The results of the West and Hunter study are shown in table 5.2

Table 5.2: Parents' Views on Coeducation

% AGREEING	CHILDREN AT		
	CO-EDUCATION	SINGLE-SEX GIRLS'	SINGLE-SEX BOYS'
No reason to separate children	81	26	39
Better preparation for life	89	29	30
Girls exert civilizing influence on boys	48	31	28
Take Equal Opportunities seriously	49	19	28
Girls' schools poorly equipped	27	7	10

Source: West and Hunter, 1993:374; summarized in Smithers and Robinson, 1995:11.

In relation to girls-only schools, there were very divergent views amongst parents of children in secondary school. These results are given in table 5.3. Those parents who had daughters at girls' schools were very sure that girls' schools allow girls to develop more personal and academic self-confidence. This view may well be due to the fact that many of the single-sex schools linked to this study were ex-grammar schools and were perceived as having 'good' academic reputations. Parents also felt that girls' schools allowed girls to develop at their own pace, which was seen to be different to the pace at which boys develop. Many parents with children at both mixed and single-sex schools seemed to agree that girls-only schools provided more examples of positive role models for girls in relation to leadership and study in traditionally male areas of the curriculum. Single-sex schools were preferred by more parents of girls than parents of boys. In fact, boys-only schools were quite unpopular. This links back to the earlier ILEA (1985) work cited above which suggested that parents of girls wished to send their girls to single-sex schools but parents of boys wished them to be educated in mixed schools. West and Hunter (1993) call for more exploratory, qualitative studies to investigate the perceptions and choices of parents further.

Table 5.3: Parents' Views on Single-sex Schooling

% AGREEING	CHILDREN AT			
	GIRLS AT SG	GIRLS AT SM	BOYS AT SB	BOYS AT SM
Girls develop more self-confidence	76	34	53	42
Examples of role models	47	43	44	56
Encourage girls to study sciences	55	27	38	50
Different rates of male/ female development	64	9	44	15

SG = secondary girls;   SM = secondary mixed;   SB = secondary boys.

Source: West and Hunter, 1993:376; also cited in Smithers and Robinson, 1995:11.

It is often the case that parents choose single-sex schooling for their daughters on religious grounds. Over the last decade, Muslims in England have been more persistent in demanding single-sex schooling for their daughters, a demand that is deeply rooted in their religious faith (Halstead, 1991). In reviewing why Muslim parents choose single-sex schooling for their daughters, Halstead shows quite perceptively that many of their arguments are similarly voiced by feminist educators in relation to single-sex schooling for girls.

For example, Halstead (op. cit.) argues that many Muslim parents choose single-sex schooling because of the wider options and choice of non-traditional stereotyped subjects for girls. There is a strong tendency for Muslim girls to opt for the natural sciences rather than arts subjects and many Muslim parents do not wish their daughters to study subjects such as home economics at school; these skills can be learnt at home. Halstead also suggests that Muslim parents want different kinds of education for girls (not necessarily an inferior education), they put considerable emphasis on women learning from each other and on women being in control of the education of girls. They also feel strongly about the level of sexual harassment experienced by girls in mixed schools and the tendency of coeducational schools not to deal adequately with this problem. Halstead (op. cit.) concludes that there is probably more common ground between all the different groups who promote single-sex schooling and prefer this sort of schooling for girls than there is difference.

Education markets

The relatively high position of single-sex girls' schools in the performance tables can be seen to have two influences on the schooling of girls. First, girls' schools seem to have had a new lease of life in relation to their popularity and second, there is now a very visible discourse of equal opportunities in mixed schools with the presence of girls being seen as a favourable characteristic for schools in the competitive, secondary school market-place (Leonard, 1996).

Ball and Gewirtz (1997) have investigated the location of girls in the education market in detail. From qualitative case studies in 14 schools they consider how girls' schools position themselves in competition with their mixed rivals (and how these mixed rivals respond) and how parents and their daughters perceive, evaluate and choose between single-sex and mixed-sex schools. Ball and Gewirtz suggest that girls' presence in schools conveys to parents choosing a school a positive impression about ethos and discipline. Girls are doing better in public examinations than boys, their presence in schools, therefore, helps in raising the position of schools in the 'league tables'.

Ball and Gewirtz (op. cit.) argue that girls' schools, in competition with mixed-sex schools, are realising that their single-sex status is their 'unique selling point' (p.212). Single-sex girls' schools in the state sector which are not only in competition with neighbouring independent girls' schools but also mixed-sex schools, are beginning more actively to stress their image, the wearing of uniform and a 'cloistered' ethos: respectability, quietness, femininity, and a particular emphasis on the performance arts:

> Traditionalism and respectability are central to and continually reinforced by the 'ethos' which these [single-sex] schools attempt to establish and communicate – an ethos strongly based on the absence of and 'escape' from boys and the forms of behaviour and relationships that girls are able to create when boys are absent... This 'cloistered' ethos was detected and commented upon positively by a number of parents we interviewed.
>
> (Ball and Gewirtz, 1997:210)

These single-sex schools also manage because of an elite 'tinge' in single-sex schooling to suggest that they parallel the private sector, i.e. they give a class coding to girls-only schools while simultaneously putting forward a form of feminism concerned with having equally high academic standards as boys (Leonard, 1996). Girls' schools thus present very complex and often conflicting messages that combine a sort of modernism and progressivism in preparing girls for careers in their own right, to be the leaders of tomorrow, with a traditionalism that emphasises femininity, safety, quietness and conformity (Ball and Gewirtz, op. cit., see table 5.4 below). Ball and Gewirtz suggest that this combination is not always successful for all girls.

Table 5.4: Traditional and Progressive Versions of Girls' Schooling

TRADITIONALISM EMPHASIZES	PROGRESSIVISM EMPHASIZES
Feminity	Feminism
Uniform	Equal opportunities
Quiet/calm	Self-assertion/confidence
Safety	Fulfilment
Away from temptation of boys	Away from domination of boys
Behaviour/discipline	Achievement
Refinements/respectability	Careers
Dance/music	Science/technology

Source: Ball and Gewirtz, 1997:220.

Mixed schools, on the other hand, now seem to be devising school-level policies, though less often practices, to encourage the recruitment of girls: 'where single-sex girls' schools exist alongside mixed competitors, the competitors find this valuable resource [girls] in short supply' (Ball and Gewirtz, 1997:214). In the competition to recruit girls, mixed-sex schools are seen to 'use' the presence of girls in their schools to market their establishments. The presence of girls in the schools is given high profile at parents' evenings, where girls can be seen fronting displays in science and technology. Also strategies are highlighted which aim to combat the rough, tough, 'macho' image of mixed schools such as single-sex teaching in certain subjects and single-sex spaces throughout the school. The schools' commitment to the arts is also emphasized and often girls are sent from mixed schools into feeder primaries to talk to younger girls about life in their mixed-sex schools.

It seems that what is emerging is an equal opportunities discourse that has sprung from the most unexpected area (Leonard, 1996).

However, Ball and Gewirtz point out that within education markets, some girls carry more 'value' than others. Some girls will achieve better in public examinations (mainly, white middle-class girls), some girls will be more expensive to educate (those with special educational needs) and some girls will be greater liabilities than others (those that display behavioural or emotional problems). In all these respects, the authors argue, gender interplays with class and with race, to contribute to the multiple complexities involved in the debate about the merits of single-sex schooling.

SINGLE-SEX CLASSES

In the past decade or so, we have seen an adoption of single-sex classes within coeducational schools as a conscious strategy to counteract the negative effects of coeducation. As commented on earlier, many mixed-schools are offering single-sex teaching groups within mixed-sex settings to try and attract girls into their schools (Ball and Gewirtz, 1997). What we are also seeing in the current panic about boys underachievement, is the strategy of single-sex teaching being used to counteract the poorer results of boys in English. These initiatives are, however, being carried out with no supporting evidence that such strategies in themselves actually improve performance nor do schools seem to be aware of any affective consequences of teaching boys and girls separately within mixed schools.

Bone (1983) states that single-sex classes within mixed schools have a long history in those subjects which were seen as more appropriate for one gender than the other. Single-sex classes have been used in subjects such as home economics, craft subjects, and PE. In the later 1980s and early 1990s, single-sex classes have been used as a way of encouraging girls to gain confidence and better performance outcomes in those subjects which have been seen as more traditionally male, particularly maths and science. In the few studies that have been carried out in relation to single-sex settings in mixed-sex schools, the results tend to show a positive effect of such settings for females as measured by improved performance and confidence in the subject in general (Gillibrand, Brawn and Osborn, 1995; Rowe, 1988).

However, improved performance and confidence were not universal in these settings (Gillibrand et al., 1995). They are often resisted within schools: there is a general perception among teachers that boys-only classes are difficult to manage and that such strategies favour girls over boys (Kenway and Willis, 1986). Moreover, Gill (1993) argues that much of the research evidence on the effects of single-sex classes is concerned with measured achievement levels rather than the effect of these strategies on pedagogy and classroom processes. Parker and Rennie (1997) also report on how often single-sex groupings are introduced into schools with little thought as to their effect on the school, the students within these groups and the teachers themselves, who often have to implement such strategies without professional development or support. They suggest that there are still major moral and ethical issues to be resolved if single-sex teaching within mixed-sex schools is to be successful.

An alternative proposal for the implementation of single-sex groupings within coeducational schools is offered by Kruse (1996) who argues that boys and girls can be both supported and challenged by periods of coeducation and sex segregation in coeducational schools. Kruse offers sex segregation as a way of decreasing the informal discrimination between the sexes. She argues that in consolidating their gender identities, the sexes demarcate themselves from each other and are forced by each other's presence to maintain their designated gender identity. In the research that Kruse has carried out (see Kruse, 1996 for an overview), single-sex groupings are used to support boys' and girls' gender identity and to challenge the existing norms of gender-appropriate behaviour. These initiatives need very skilled teaching and good staff development programmes, but what they offer is an important opportunity for pupils to discover for themselves what is different about the single-sex setting and how the patterns change when they go back into mixed settings.

6
Summary, conclusions and future research agenda

SUMMARY AND CONCLUSIONS

This review has considered the most recent evidence to date on the educational achievement of girls in single-sex schools. In doing so, it looked not only at how girls are achieving in these schools, but also how they are achieving in relation to boys generally and how other aspects of single-sex schooling might be attractive to girls and parents of daughters. Over the last decade there has been an increase in the popularity of single-sex schooling for girls. However, this is in contrast to a considerable decrease in the number of single-sex schools available in the UK in both the state and independent sectors.

In reviewing the most recent literature, this report has shown that the findings presented in the wide-ranging EOC study of 1983 are reinforced by many of the more recent studies that have focused on girls' achievements and the effects of single-sex and coeducational schools:

- the pattern of differences and similarities in academic performance of girls and boys suggests that the performance of a school in terms of examination results has much less to do with whether it is single-sex or not than with other factors;

- the better performances of girls' schools are not strictly related to single-sexness but to differences in intake that relate to social class and ability, and the histories and traditions of the schools;

- social class and prior attainment remain the most powerful predictors of educational achievement;

- there are bigger differences between the type of school, i.e. whether it is independent, selective or comprehensive, than whether it is single-sex or not;

- certain schools show differential effectiveness for certain sub-groups of pupils, with coeducation having a stronger impact on lower ability boys and girls;

- girls' schools in both the independent and state sectors are well placed in the performance tables because girls do better than boys generally in examinations at the end of compulsory schooling;

- these patterns of results and findings from research studies carried out in the UK are supported by similar studies carried out in other developed countries.

However, academic achievement is only one of the goals of schooling and parents, teachers and pupils themselves may differ about the extent of its importance. Academic achievement is only one aspect of the complex debate about single-sex schooling and the report aims to highlight some of those factors which explain why single-sex schooling is seen as desirable and beneficial for some girls.

Educational experience

- Much of the research evidence continues to show very different school experiences for boys and for girls. There was evidence to suggest that single-sex schools and classes did much for the promotion of girls' confidence and self esteem and that single-sex spaces allowed girls to get a clearer picture of their own abilities and contribution to classroom learning.

Pupils' views of schooling

- There was evidence to suggest that pupils themselves felt that attendance at single-sex schools was academically beneficial whereas attendance at coeducational schools was socially beneficial. This perception tended to hold whether attendance was at these school types in the independent or state sector. Pupils in coeducational schools have a more positive view of their schools' impact on their social and personal development and have less traditional views about work and family roles, but girls still have heavier domestic workloads than boys irrespective of the type of school they attend.

- Evidence from girls who had attended single-sex schools suggested that they tended to fear there might have been distractions had there been boys present, seemed to value having been pushed academically, yet voiced reservations about single-sex environments for girls being too competitive, and prone to spitefulness. In contrast to this, girls who had attended co-educational schools regarded teaching the sexes together as the natural thing to do and rejected the idea that boys had dominated the lessons in their schools. They also agreed that it was better to have both male and female perspectives when studying in the sixth form, and that their experience of coeducational schooling had made it easier to adjust to life in higher education.

Subject choice

- Much of the evidence does suggest that there are more polarised choices of subjects amongst girls and boys at coeducational schools than at single-sex schools and that subjects such as maths and science are more popular amongst girls in single-sex schools and music and languages more popular amongst boys at single-sex schools. However, again the evidence was not conclusive and tended to show that the school effect in terms of choice of subject was not present amongst older pupils. The polarisation of subject choice continued for both boys and girls into advanced level study and also the study of vocational subjects.

Parental choice

- Differences have been found between those parents who send their children to coeducational schools and those who choose single-sex schools. Parents sending their children to coeducational schools see no reason for separating the sexes and believe it is a better preparation for adult life. Parents preferring single-sex education tend to believe that in the absence of boys girls develop more self-confidence, are more likely to encounter female role models in leadership and traditionally male subjects and are less likely to choose stereotyped subjects. The paradox that is generated from the data is that many parents wish their daughters to be educated in single-sex schools and their sons in mixed schools.

Girls in the education market-place

- In the present climate of competition amongst schools, single-sex girls schools are using their single-sexness as their 'unique selling point' and in doing so advertise an offering to parents that is on the one hand traditional (wearing of uniform, quiet spaces, femininity) and on the other progressive (wide range of subjects, educating the women of tomorrow, feminism). The common element from both sides of this combination is the absence of boys. However, evidence shows that this combination of traditionalism and progressivism is not always successful for all girls.

- Mixed schools are devising school-level policies to encourage the recruitment of girls, as for many mixed-sex schools this valuable commodity is in short supply. Mixed-sex schools are 'using' the presence and success of girls to sell their schools and are trying to combat the rough, tough, 'macho' image of the mixed school and promote all-girls' classes and spaces in order to attract girls into their schools. What is emerging is an equal opportunities discourse that has sprung from the most unexpected area. However, what is still clear is that some girls are more 'valuable' than others in the education market place.

Single-sex classes

- There has been a marked increase in the popularity of single-sex classes within coeducation to counteract some of the negative effects of coeducational schooling. There is some evidence to suggest that the teaching of girls in single-sex classes has a positive effect on their confidence and academic performance. However, often these strategies have been implemented more as 'quick fixes' to particular educational problems (e.g. the underachievement of boys) than as well thought out programmes that are supported by staff development programmes and include reflection on sex segregation and coeducation by the pupils involved.

The general conclusion from this review is that there is no conclusive evidence to suggest that single-sex schooling is better than coeducational schooling. Too many variables are involved to support such a suggestion. While we do not wish to detract from the obvious successes of girls' schools in the performance tables, the research evidence continues to support the view that there is no general rule that one type of school is better than the other. There are many personal, social, cultural and religious reasons why parents choose either single-sex or coeducational schooling for their children. In choosing the best school for their child, the research reviewed for this study suggests that parents must make their choice in relation to the child's needs and preferences in combination with their own preferences and the reputation of the school.

FUTURE RESEARCH AGENDA

There are some clear areas where research is needed if we are to have a fuller picture of how the range of girls who attend single-sex schools achieve and what their educational experiences are. The following is a list of those areas that could be the focus of future research studies:

- There is very little data or research on the range of girls' schools in the state sector. Research on the 'unique qualities' of existing maintained girls' schools would be useful, both in itself, and in the design of future studies.

- Most of the research reported in this review is of a cross-sectional nature and tends to ignore the students' voice. Further research is needed that takes a longitudinal look at the effects of single-sex schooling, how it prepares girls for life in mixed-sex universities and the labour market in general and how girls themselves experience these different phases of education.

- There is very little data which looks at the interaction of gender, race and class and the performance of girls. It would be of considerable interest to know how the interaction of these three variables affects performance in single-sex schools as well as coeducational schools.

- Many of the studies which investigate student performance are looking at those students who succeed in school and who are entered for examinations: they concern themselves mostly with successful girls. There is an obvious need to look more closely at those girls who drop out and for whom education is a negative experience. What influences their decisions and what makes them choose not to participate need to be areas of focus in qualitative studies of all-girls' schools.

NOTE

[1]   At the time of wrting this report (June 1998) the national curriculum has changed again from that which was implemented in the early 1990s, with more choice brought back in and the possibility of taking general vocational qualifications at 16. However, 16-year-old boys and girls still have to take English, maths and science as compulsory subjects at the end of secondary schooling.

REFERENCES

American Association of University Women (AAUW) (1992), *How Schools Shortchange Girls*. Washington DC: AAUW Educational Foundation/National Education Foundation.

— (1998), *Separated By Sex: A Critical Look at Single-Sex Education for Girls*. Washington DC: AAUW Educational Foundation.

Arnot, M. (1983), 'A cloud over coeducation: an analysis of the forms of transmission of class and gender relation'. In S. Walker and L. Barton (eds), *Gender, Class and Education*. London: Falmer Press.

Arnot, M., David, M. and Weiner, G. (1996), *Educational Reforms and Gender Equality in Schools*. Manchester: Equal Opportunities Commission.

Arnot, M., Gray, J., James, M., Rudduck, J. and Duveen, G. (1998), *Review of Recent Research on Gender and Educational Performance*. London: HMSO.

Baker, P., Riordan, C. and Schaub, M. (1995), 'The effects of sex-grouped schooling on achievement: the role of national context', *Comparative Education Review*, 39(4):468-482.

Ball, S. J. and Gewirtz, S. (1997), 'Girls in the education market: choice, competition and complexity', *Gender and Education*, 9(2):207-222.

Barber, M. (1994), *Young People and Their Attitudes to School: Interim Report*. Centre for Successful Schools, Keele University.

Bone, A. (1983), *Girls and Girls'-Only Schools*. Manchester: Equal Opportunities Commission.

Bright, M. (1998), 'Boys performing badly', *The Observer*, January 4th 1998.

Burgess, A. (1990), 'Co-education – the disadvantages for girls', *Gender and Education*, 2(1):91-95.

Carpenter, P. (1985), 'Single-sex schooling and girls' academic achievements', *Australian and New Zealand Journal of Sociology*, 21(3).

Colley, A., Comber, C. and Hargreaves, D. (1994), 'School subject preferences of pupils in single-sex and co-educational secondary schools', *Educational Studies*, 20(3):379-385.

Dale, R. R. (1969, 1971, 1974), *Mixed or Single-Sex School Vols I-III*. London: Routledge and Kegan Paul.

Daly, P. (1996), 'The effects of single-sex and coeducational secondary schooling on girls' achievement', *Research Papers in Education*, 11(3):289-306.

Deem, R. (1984), *Co-education Reconsidered*. Milton Keynes: Open University Press.

Elwood, J. (1995), 'Undermining gender stereotypes: examination and coursework performance in the UK at 16', *Assessment in Education*, 2(3):283-303.

Equal Opportunities Commission (EOC) and Office for Standards in Education (Ofsted) (1996), *The Gender Divide: Performance differences between boys and girls at school*. London: HMSO.

Felstead, A. (1998), A Statistical Portrait of Underachievement by Gender: The National Targets for Education and Training. Paper presented at QCA Research Seminar on Underachievement, London, June 1998

Gallagher, A., McKwen, A. and Knipe, D. (1996), *Girls and 'A' Level Science 1985 to 1995: Report for the Equal Opportunities for Northern Ireland*. Belfast: The Equal Opportunities Commission.

Gallagher, A. (1997), *Educational Achievement and Gender: A review of research evidence on the apparent underachievement of boys*. Belfast, NI: DENI.

Gender Working Party (1994), *Men's and Women's Performance in Tripos Examinations 1980-1993*. Cambridge: University of Cambridge.

Gill, J. (1993), 'Re-phrasing the question about single sex schooling'. In A. Reid and B. Johnson (eds), *Critical Issues in Australian Education in the 1990s*. Adelaide: Painters Prints.

Gillborn, D. and Gipps, C. (1996), *Recent Review on the Achievements of Ethnic Minority Pupils*. London: HMSO.

Gillibrand, E., Brawn, R. and Osborn, A. (1995), Girls' Confidence, Achievement and Participation in All-Girls' Classes in Mixed Schools. Unpublished paper from Bristol University, School of Education.

Halstead, M. (1991). 'Radical feminism, Islam and the single-sex school debate', *Gender and Education*, 3(3):263-278.

Hannan, D. F., Smyth, E., McCullagh, J., O'Leary, R. and McMahon, D. (1996), *Coeducation and gender equality: exam performance, stress and personal development*. Dublin: Oak Tree Press.

Harris, S., Nixon, J. and Rudduck, J. (1993), 'School work, homework and gender', *Gender and Education*, 5(1):3-15.

Haw, K. F. (1994), 'Muslim girls' schools – a conflict of interests?', *Gender and Education*, 6(1):63-76.

Inner London Education Authority (ILEA) (1985), *Report of the Work of the Working Party on Single-sex and Co-education*. ILEA 5521.

— (1990a), *How Equal? Monitoring Equal Opportunities in Education, 1981-89*. RS 1279/90.

— (1990b), *Differences in Examination Performance*. RS 1277/90.

Jiminez, E. and Lockheed, M. (1989), 'Relative effectiveness of single-sex and coeducational schools in Thailand', *Educational Evaluation and Policy Analysis*, 11:117-42.

Judd, J. (1994), They're falling rapidly behind girls at school. Are boys in terminal decline?', *The Independent*, October 18th 1994.

Kenway, J. and Willis, S. (1986), 'Feminist single-sex educational strategies: some theoretical flaws and practical fallacies', *Discourse*, 7(1):1-30.

Kruse, A. M. (1996), 'Single-sex settings: pedagogies for girls and boys in Danish schools'. In P. Murphy and C. Gipps (eds), *Equity in the Classroom: Towards Effective Pedagogy for Girls and Boys*. London/ Paris: The Falmer Press/UNESCO:173-191.

Lee, V. R. and Bryk, A. S. (1986), 'Effects of single-sex secondary schools on student achievement and attitudes', *Journal of Educational Psychology*, 78:381-95.

Lee, V. E. and Lockheed, M. (1990), 'The effects of single-sex schooling on achievement and attitudes in Nigeria', *Comparative Education Review*, 34:209-31.

Leonard, D. (1996), 'The debate around co-education'. In S. Kemal, D. Leonard, M. Pringle and S. Sadeque (eds), *Targeting Underachievement: Boys or Girls?* London: Institute of Education/ CREG):21-29.

Lepkowska, D. (1998), 'Whatever happened to the likely lads?' *Times Educational Supplement*, January 9th 1998.

Mahony, P. (1985), *Schools for the Boys? Co-education Reassessed*. London: Hutchinson.

Marsh, H. W. (1989), 'The effects of attending single-sex and coeducational high schools on achievement, attitudes an behaviours and on sex differences', *Journal of Educational Psychology*, 81:70-85.

McCrum, N. G. (1996), 'Gender and Social Inequality at Oxford and Cambridge Universities', *Oxford Review of Education*, 22(4):369-398.

Nuttall, D., Thomas, S. and Goldstein, H. (1992), *Report on Analysis of 1990 Examination Results*. AMA EO Circular 92/13.

Parker, L. and Rennie, L. (1997), 'Teachers' perceptions of the implementation of single-sex classes in coeducational schools', *Australian Journal of Education,* 41(2):119-133.

Pyke, N. (1996), 'Why the girls are on top', *Times Educational Supplement,* March 22nd 1996

Riordan, C. (1985), 'Public and catholic schooling: the effects of gender context policy', *American Journal of Education,* 93:518-40.

Rowe, K. J. (1988), 'Single-sex and mixed-sex classes: the effects of class type on student achievement, confidence and participation in mathematics', *Australian Journal of Education,* 32(2):180-202.

Rudduck, J., Chaplain, R. and Wallace, G. (1996), *School Improvement: What Can Pupils Tell Us?* London: David Fulton Publishers.

Sadker, M. and Sadker, D. (1993), *Failing at Fairness.* New York: Charles Scribner's Sons.

Sammons, P. (1995), 'Differences in attainment', *British Educational Research Journal,* 21(4):485.

Sammons, P., Nuttall, D., Cuttance, P. and Thomas, S. (1994), *Continuity of School Effects.* London: Institute of Education.

Shaw, J. (1976), 'Finishing school: some implications of sex segregated education', In D. Baker and S. Allen (eds), *Sexual Divisions in Society: Process and Change.* London: Tavistock.

Smithers, A. and Robinson, P. (1995), *Co-educational and Single-Sex Schooling.* Manchester: Centre for Education and Employment Research, University of Manchester.

— (1997) *Co-education and Single-sex – Revisited.* Uxbridge: Brunel University.

Spender, D. (1980), *Man Made Learning.* London: Routledge and Kegan Paul.

Stables, A. (1990), 'Differences between pupils from mixed and single-sex schools in their enjoyment of school subjects and in their attitudes to science and to school', *Educational Review*, 42(3):221-230.

Stables, A. and Stables, S. (1995), 'Gender differences in students' approaches to A-level subject choices and perceptions of A-level subjects: a study of first-year A-level students in a tertiary college', *Educational Research*, 37(1):39-51.

Steedman, J. (1984), *Examination results in Mixed and Single-Sex Schools: Findings from the National Child Development Study.* Manchester: Equal Opportunities Commission.

Steedman, J. (1985), 'Examination results in mixed and single-sex secondary schools'. In D. Reynolds (ed.), *Studying School Effectiveness.* London: Falmer.

Stobart, G., White, J., Elwood, J., Hayden, M. and Mason, K. (1992), *Differential Performance in Examinations at 16+: English and Mathematics.* London: Schools Examination and Assessment Council.

Thomas, S., Nuttall, D. and Goldstein, H. (1993), *Report on Analysis of 1991 Examination Results.* AMA EO Circular 93/24.

Thomas, S., Pan, H. and Goldstein, H. (1994), *Report on Analysis of 1992 Examination Results.* London : AMA and Institute of Education.

Thomas, S. and Elliot, K. (1996, 1997), *A Contextualised Analysis of the Summer 1996 and 1997 Baseline Assessments: Sample of Feedback to Schools.* London: Institute of Education.

Turner, E., Riddell, S. and Brown, S. (1995), *Gender Equality in Scottish Schools.* Glasgow: Equal Opportunities Commission.

West, A. and Hunter, J. (1993), 'Parents' Views on Mixed and Single-sex Secondary School, *British Journal of Educational Research*, 19(4):369-380.

Yates, L. (1983), *The Education of Girls: Policy Research and the Question of Gender.* Hawthorn, Victoria: The Australian Council for Educational Research.